This is from your
Favorite
Christian Relation

It will help you
with some of the things
Jesus has done for you.
Love
Mike

101

THINGS

JESUS
HAS DONE
for YOU

A SIMPLE CELEBRATION OF THE MANY BLESSINGS
WE RECEIVE THROUGH THE GIFT OF KNOWING JESUS!

Published by

THOMAS NELSON
Since 1798

www.thomasnelson.com

Table of Contents

Introduction

While Jesus was on earth, many people traveled great distances to catch even a distant glimpse of the Nazarene who was said to be the Messiah. They wanted to know more about Him and find out if the rumors were true.

The same happens in our own lives. When we hear about Jesus—when we hear about what He does in the lives of ordinary people—we want to find out more about Him.

What we find is that knowing Jesus offers blessings beyond our wildest dreams. And even if we've known Him many years, we find that He is always astonishing us with new ways of meeting our needs and restoring our souls.

Sometimes we need a moment to reflect, to be still and let our minds wander over the many things Jesus has done for us, to let the truth of His goodness take hold in our hearts. We need to rekindle our gratitude by remembering the blessings of Christ. We need to receive His peace by reflecting on His great power and love.

In the following pages, you'll find reflections and Scriptures that remind us of what Jesus does in our lives. Linger as He forgives a sinful woman and heals Blind Bartimaeus. Watch as He quiets the storm. And celebrate as He takes on the sin of the world and defeats death, remembering how He took on your sin and rescued you from the bleakness of your life before you met Him.

Read and remember, and let your heart be filled with wonder.

1

Therefore, there is now no condemnation for those who are in Christ Jesus, because through Christ Jesus the law of the Spirit of life set me free from the law of sin and death.

ROMANS 8:1–2

JESUS GIVES US A CLEAN SLATE.

We know the feeling well: guilt. It has followed us during the day and kept us awake at night. We can't forget the things we've done, no matter how much we may want to.

The good news is that in Christ, God accepts us as His children. We can be free from guilt knowing that He has forgiven us—completely. "Though your sins are like scarlet," He tells us, "they shall be as white as snow" (Isaiah 1:18b). And while we still face the consequences of our sin and sometimes the discipline of our Heavenly Father, we can finally sleep at night, resting in the assurance that God is *for* us.

2

My command is this: Love each other as I have loved you.
JOHN 15:12

JESUS LOVES US.

We watch Jesus loving people throughout the Gospels. Sometimes His love is exasperated, like when He laments over Jerusalem, "How often I have longed to gather your children together, as a hen gathers her chicks under her wings, but you were not willing!" (Luke 13:34b). Sometimes it is challenging, like when He challenges the rich young ruler to give up what was most important to him. And sometimes His love is simply indescribable, like when He stretches out His arms and allows Himself to be crucified.

Jesus loves us with an everlasting love. And He shows us His love in many ways throughout our lives—but never more plainly or powerfully than dying on the cross.

3

Therefore, brothers, since we have confidence to enter the Most Holy
Place by the blood of Jesus, . . . let us draw near to God with a sincere
heart in full assurance of faith, having our hearts sprinkled to cleanse us
from a guilty conscience and having our bodies washed with pure water.

HEBREWS 10:19, 22

JESUS GIVES US CONFIDENCE BEFORE OUR HEAVENLY FATHER.

In the Temple in Jerusalem, only a priest could enter the
Most Holy Place, and only on the Day of Atonement, when
he made the annual offering for sins. But when Jesus died,
the Temple curtain was torn in two. The wall between us and
God was shattered.

Because of Jesus, anytime we have need, without ritual or
special dispensation, we can come into the presence of God.
We can come boldly, with confidence that we will be received
by the Father who adopted us through His Son's blood.
Because of the relationship with God we have through Jesus,
we can approach Him with a free, untroubled heart.

4

I have come that they may have life, and have it to the full.

JOHN 10:10B

JESUS GIVES US A RICH, ABUNDANT LIFE.

In a hot, oppressive desert, sheep are vulnerable to the elements and predators. They need a shepherd who can lead them to water and food each day and keep them safe each night.

Jesus tells us that He is that Shepherd. Unlike the thief, who "comes only to steal and kill and destroy," Jesus has come that we may "have life, and have it to the full" (John 10:10). He knows us by name and is committed to our care. Life as one of Jesus' sheep is indeed full—full of His abundant love, faithful attention, and amazing grace.

Whether you turn to the right or to the left, your ears will hear a voice
behind you, saying, "This is the way; walk in it."

ISAIAH 30:21

JESUS GIVES US HIS GUIDANCE.

Every journey needs either a roadmap or a navigator.
Fortunately for us, in our journey with Jesus, we have both.

We have the Scriptures to tell us where we are in God's
redemptive plan, how to participate in that plan, and how to
order our lives. The Bible tells us who God is and how to
interact with Him, as well as how to interact with others and
share God's grace with them. And when Jesus left the earth,
He left us a "navigator"—the Holy Spirit guides us into all
truth and leads and directs us.

Jesus hasn't left us without a guide. He watches over our
every step.

8

In all these things we are more than conquerors through him who loved us. For I am convinced that neither death nor life, neither angels nor demons, neither the present nor the future, nor any powers, neither height nor depth, nor anything else in all creation, will be able to separate us from the love of God that is in Christ Jesus our Lord.

ROMANS 8:37–39

JESUS MAKES US OVERCOMERS.

James tells us to "consider it pure joy, my brothers, whenever you face trials of many kinds, because you know that the testing of your faith develops perseverance" (1:2–3). That's a tough thing to do. But it gets easier when we remember that "we are more than conquerors through him who loved us" (Romans 8:37b), because we know what lies on the other side of every trial: the love of God.

"If God is for us, who can be against us?" Paul asks. Since God has loved us so lavishly in Christ, what do we have to fear? His love is more than enough to overcome any trial.

9

He himself bore our sins in his body on the tree, so that we might die to
sins and live for righteousness; by his wounds you have been healed.

1 PETER 2:24

JESUS HEALS US OF
THE SICKNESS OF SIN.

Not everyone has experienced a long-term physical illness—
waiting for test results, living with questions about what the
days ahead will bring, wondering if the physical discomfort
will ever go away. But we have all suffered from a spiritual
illness. We have all known the sickness of sin.

When Jesus steps into our lives, darkness gives way to light,
our hardened hearts becoming softer. We're filled with the
joy of knowing God and the desire to please Him. And as the
choking grip of sin begins to slip away, we are empowered and
enabled to live right with God.

10

Beloved, we are God's children now; what we will be has not yet been
revealed. What we do know is this; when he is revealed,
we will be like him, for we will see him as he is.

1 JOHN 3:2 NRSV

JESUS MAKES US MORE LIKE HIM.

Watching old TV shows or movies is more fun when they
feature someone who went on to become famous. In their
younger faces, when they smile or squint a certain way, we can
see traces of who they will become.

In the same way, we bear traces of Jesus. When we first began
our journey with Him, He began working in us, making us
more and more like Him. And He has continued that work in
our lives, slowly chiseling us after His image of longsuffering,
kindness, and holiness. As we walk with Christ, we grow into
His image more and more every day.

11

I can do everything through him who gives me strength.
PHILIPPIANS 4:13

JESUS GIVES US HIS UNLIMITED STRENGTH.

When we first set out to do something difficult and challenging, we wonder if we'll have enough strength to finish it. Will our lungs hold out, or will we collapse halfway up the mountain? Will we be able to see our loved one through an illness, or will we lose heart?

Paul's exultation in Philippians 4:12–13 is that no matter what task was set before him or what trials he endured, he had found the strength of Christ to be completely sufficient. He could do all things through His perfect strength. Christ is always, Paul's life declares, completely *enough*.

12

We are His workmanship, created in Christ Jesus for good works,
which God prepared beforehand that we should walk in them.
EPHESIANS 2:10 NKJV

JESUS GIVES OUR LIVES MEANING AND PURPOSE.

A hammer isn't quite a hammer unless it's hammering. And we're not quite fulfilled unless we're doing something that has meaning and a purpose higher than ourselves.

Jesus has invited us to be part of the coming Kingdom—and He's given us each a personal mission to further that Kingdom. He told His disciples, "You will receive power when the Holy Spirit comes upon you; and you will be my witnesses in Jerusalem, and in all Judea and Samaria and to the ends of the earth" (Acts 1:8). Jesus has given us a job to do—one that makes our lives full, exciting, and eternally significant.

I have said these things to you so that my joy may be in you,
and that your joy may be full.

JOHN 15:11 NRSV

JESUS GIVES US THE GIFT OF JOY.

With a vaguely European accent, a man in a coffeeshop was overheard to say to his friend, "So how are you? Is there any dancing in your world today?"

As Jesus prepared His disciples for His crucifixion, their world was shrouded in uncertainty. So He comforted them, telling them of His love for them and saying, "I have told you this so that my joy may be in you" (John 15:11a). When fear and doubt cloud our world, we too can count on His love to renew our joy.

Because of the love of Jesus, there is dancing in our world every day. No matter what circumstances we're facing, we always have a reason to celebrate and be glad.

14

In his great mercy he has given us new birth into a living hope through the resurrection of Jesus Christ from the dead.

1 PETER 1:3B

JESUS OFFERS US AN UNDYING HOPE.

Any runner knows that finishing a race is mostly mental. Without the knowledge that he can complete the distance before him, his mind starts to weaken, and his body soon follows. Likewise, when our spiritual endurance is tested, the deciding factor is whether or not our hope will hold out. If hope dies, our spirits are crushed, and we lose the will to continue.

Thankfully, the hope we have in Jesus will never die, because He lives forever. We know—beyond a shadow of a doubt—that He will ultimately triumph in our lives and in the world. Because He lives, we have hope.

Peace I leave with you; my peace I give you.
JOHN 14:27A

JESUS GIVES US THE GIFT OF PEACE.

While He was on earth, Jesus' hands did many things. They touched lepers and made them well. They blessed bread and multiplied the loaves. And they stretched over a stormy sea and quieted the waves.

Even now, Jesus' hands stretch over our lives, giving us His peace and stilling the storms of our hearts. We experience His peace when we pray and when we read about Him, remembering His great power and His great love for us. And sometimes we experience His peace in a way that transcends our understanding, in an unexplainable calm that wraps itself around us, a gift from our loving Savior.

16

And my God will meet all your needs according to
his glorious riches in Christ Jesus.
PHILIPPIANS 4:19

JESUS PROVIDES FOR
ALL OUR NEEDS.

It came at just the right time—the check would fill in the
gaps that month during a season of unemployment. It was a
gift from a church friend and a symbol of God's provision.

God calls us to give generously. He also calls us to give
fearlessly, knowing that He is more than able and more than
willing to meet our every need. The truth is that when we give
lavishly, we're giving as God gives—He lavishes us with love
and blessings in Christ. With Him as our shepherd, we surely
shall not want.

17

He who has the Son has life.
1 JOHN 5:12A

JESUS GIVES US LIFE.

We see death all around us every day. Just watch the news for an eyeful of murders, bombings, and tragic accidents. And it's not just physical death that plagues us. If we knew the life stories of the people we interact with every day, we might be shocked by the pain that infects their souls.

In the midst of all this death and darkness, Jesus brings life and light. Where there is destruction, He restores. Where there is hurt, He heals. Where there is death, He resurrects. He replaces our ashes with beauty and our mourning with gladness. In a dying world, Jesus brings life.

18

For every child of God defeats this evil world,
and we achieve this victory through our faith.
1 JOHN 5:4 NLT

JESUS GIVES US VICTORY.

"Victory" is a good sports word. Victory is about vanquishing a foe, achieving success in a battle.

Whether or not we've ever played pro ball, we all know about battling foes, because we all battle our sinful nature every day. It's hard to love the way God loves and follow the commands He left us. But with the power of Christ within us, we can overcome our sinfulness, and we can participate in God's glorious plan to conquer evil—for good. No matter how much we may feel like the underdog, Jesus in us ensures our victory.

19

He who did not spare His own Son, but delivered Him up for us all,
how shall He not with Him also freely give us all things.

ROMANS 8:32 NKJV

JESUS BLESSES US BEYOND OUR IMAGINATION.

It's true that the road is narrow; following Jesus is not a life of luxury. But it's also true that God has numbered the hairs on our head, and that "no eye has seen, no ear has heard, no mind has conceived what God has prepared for those who love him" (1 Corinthians 2:9b).

We can count on God's provision and blessings because He's already proven His faithfulness by providing His Son. Because of Jesus, we can approach our days with faith and watchfulness. We never know how God might bless us today.

Truly our fellowship *is* with the Father and with His Son Jesus Christ.
1 JOHN 1:3B NKJV

JESUS GIVES US A RELATIONSHIP WITH GOD.

Few things in life are as vital to our soul as relationship. We need to meet with other people to share our lives and help each other along. Besides, relationships are often what make life fun and exciting.

So it should amaze us that through Jesus, God has offered us a relationship with Him. Because of Jesus, we have access to a holy God and can enjoy Him as our Father and Friend. We can talk with Him twenty-four hours a day and be assured that He hears us. Our relationship with God brings our lives contentment and joy—and it's all because of Jesus.

21

And surely I am with you always, to the very end of the age.
MATTHEW 28:20B

JESUS GIVES US THE GIFT OF HIS PRESENCE.

When we were learning to ride a bike, knowing that Dad was holding the back of the seat made us feel confident and capable. When we sit in a waiting room, the wordless presence of friends and family sustains us and calms us. There's something about knowing that someone is beside us that makes challenges and difficulties bearable.

Jesus tells us that He is that Someone, that He will always be with us. He feels the pain we feel and shares our joys. He cheers our victories and comforts us in defeat. He is beside us every step of the way.

Come to me, all you who are weary and burdened,
and I will give you rest. Take my yoke upon you and learn from me,
for I am gentle and humble in heart, and you will find rest for your souls.
For my yoke is easy and my burden is light.

MATTHEW 11:28–30

JESUS GIVES US REST.

It's hard to walk with heavy baggage weighing us down. And all of us have "weights" that we carry throughout our lives—burdens of guilt, fear, sadness, and anger.

Jesus promises that if we trade our burdens in for His, He will give our souls rest. In Jesus, we can finally set down the weights we've been dragging behind us and simply rest in His gentleness and strength.

Paul tells us to "carry each other's burdens, and in this way you will fulfill the law of Christ" (Galatians 6:2). When we strengthen and care for each other, we are acting like Jesus. Because that's exactly what He does for us.

Therefore, since we have been justified through faith,
we have peace with God through our Lord Jesus Christ.
ROMANS 5:1

Jesus gives us peace with God.

When families or friends dispute, there is always a cutting anxiety, an unspoken fear that the relationship will never be mended. And sometimes, as weeks turn into months and years without an olive branch, that fear becomes realized.

When Jesus came to earth, He destroyed everything that came between us and God by dying on the cross. No longer are we at enmity with God—we now have full access to Him and the opportunity for a close, thriving, ongoing relationship with Him.

Jesus is the olive branch that stills our fear and grants peace to our lives, knowing that we are on good terms with God.

Therefore I will boast all the more gladly about my weaknesses,
so that Christ's power may rest on me. That is why, for Christ's sake,
I delight in weaknesses, in insults, in hardships, in persecutions, in
difficulties. For when I am weak, then I am strong.

2 CORINTHIANS 12:9B–10

JESUS GIVES US HIS MIGHTY POWER IN OUR WEAKNESS.

Weakness is to be avoided at all costs, we tell ourselves. When we discover a weakness, we usually cover it up with excuses and blame-shifting and use our strengths to overshadow our flaws. There's something in us that's terrified of being insufficient, of needing someone else.

The truth is that we are all, at some time or another, weak. Sometimes we can't make it on our own. We fail. But Paul's amazing and somewhat paradoxical declaration is that the end of our strength is the best place in the world to be—because that's exactly where our mighty Savior steps in. His perfect strength works perfectly in our weakness.

Through him you believe in God, who raised him from the dead and
glorified him, and so your faith and hope are in God.

1 PETER 1:21

JESUS GIVES US FAITH AND HOPE.

More than once, the disciples turned to Jesus, alarmed and
fearful. On one such occasion, a storm sprang up suddenly,
and they were caught in rough seas. They woke Jesus, saying,
"Teacher, don't you care if we drown?" (Mark 4:38b). He
responded by calming the storm with a simple word. And
then he asked them, "Why are you so afraid? Do you still
have no faith?" (Mark 4:40b).

When we hold onto faith in Jesus, we have no need to fear
for our future. Through Him, we have hope in the One who
holds everything in His hands. Our faith and hope in God—
our dependence on Him for the future—is the most abiding
and sustaining hope we'll ever find.

26

So in Christ we who are many form one body,
and each member belongs to all the others.

ROMANS 12:5

JESUS BRINGS US INTO A FAMILY OF BELIEVERS.

Few things lift our souls like the energy that crackles among people who belong together. A sense of belonging is one of the most deeply felt human needs. But even though we were made for community, lots of things conspire to prick holes in our relationships, and many of us feel alone.

Jesus offers a remedy for our loneliness by calling us to be part of His Body. In Him we find acceptance—and His love fills our hearts and spreads to those around us. And while we may face obstacles on the road to true fellowship, we have the promise of Jesus' powerful love to comfort us and draw us closer to others.

27

It is because of him that you are in Christ Jesus, who has become for us wisdom from God—that is, our righteousness, holiness and redemption.

1 CORINTHIANS 1:30

JESUS GIVES US THE GIFT OF WISDOM.

Proverbs tells us, "Wisdom is supreme; therefore get wisdom" (4:7a). Wisdom is priceless, the Bible teaches, because it enables us to make choices that honor God and help us lead a richer life.

The truth about wisdom is that it has little to do with college degrees and hours of study. Wisdom is God centered—its purpose is to direct us to depend on Him and order our lives around Him. As much as we might try to make ourselves wise, wisdom is ultimately the gift of God.

In Christ, we have all the resources and guidance we'll ever need to make wise, godly choices. In Christ we find the fullness of wisdom.

28

So we, too, have put our faith in Christ Jesus that we may be
justified by faith in Christ and not by observing the law,
because by observing the law no one will be justified.

GALATIANS 2:16B

JESUS GIVES US THE GIFT OF RIGHTEOUSNESS.

In the Old Testament, God's "righteousness" often means
His faithfulness to the covenant He made with Israel. God
in His righteousness is completely loyal—He always follows
through.

The same can't be said about us. We regularly miss the mark.
We cheat on God; we fail to reflect His glory and uphold His
standards.

Fortunately, in Christ, God gives us His righteousness. He
counts us righteous in Christ, giving us an unblemished
record, and He makes us more holy, more faithful to Him and
His ways of living. Clothed in the righteousness of Christ, we
live in a loving, connected, faithful covenant with God.

29

Praise be to the God and Father of our Lord Jesus Christ, who has blessed
us in the heavenly realms with every spiritual blessing in Christ.

EPHESIANS 1:3

JESUS GIVES US EVERY SPIRITUAL BLESSING.

It's human nature: We can't help but guard our lives
protectively, even at times territorially. Like vines climbing
toward sunlight, we desperately want to thrive. And when
following Christ means trusting Him and depending on Him
rather than ourselves, sometimes we balk.

But our fears settle when we remember that God has blessed
us "in the heavenly realms with every spiritual blessing in
Christ" (Ephesians 1:3b). There is nothing we need that is
beyond Christ's sufficiency, and there is nothing on earth that
can destroy or diminish the blessings God holds for us "in the
heavenly realms." When we depend on Jesus, we thrive more
completely, more abundantly than we ever could on our own.

30

But now in Christ Jesus you who once were far away have been brought
near through the blood of Christ.

EPHESIANS 2:13

JESUS BRINGS US NEAR TO GOD.

In a certain sense, Paul tells us, we've all been Gentiles at
one time in our lives or another: We've all been outside the
purposes of God, "without hope and without God in the
world" (Ephesians 2:12b). Our hearts were far away from
Him, our lives a crazy mess of trying to figure things out on
our own.

But in Christ, God has brought us near to Himself. We are
His children, and He holds us close enough to hear His voice
speaking to us and guiding us, to hear His heartbeat. We're
no longer struggling on our own, no longer without hope. We
have the privilege of living close to God.

31

Do not be anxious about anything, but in everything, by prayer and
petition, with thanksgiving, present your requests to God.
And the peace of God, which transcends all understanding,
will guard your hearts and your minds in Christ Jesus.

PHILIPPIANS 4:6–7

JESUS FREES US FROM ANXIETY.

Anxiety is the chief enemy of peace. Anxiety threatens our
sleep and our sanity. And it's when we're anxious that we're
most likely to lash out at others, ruining our peace with them
and with ourselves.

Jesus soothes our anxiety by offering us His peace. Our
anxiety can be overcome, Paul tells us, by praying—removing
our anxieties from our heart, where they stir us and trouble
us, and placing them in His hands. As we do so, God's peace
will flow from heaven, soothing our spirits, even if we can't
understand why we have the peace that we do. In Christ, our
hearts and minds are guarded, safe and secure from every
threat to peace.

32

Keep your eyes on Jesus, who both began and finished this race we're in.
HEBREWS 12:2A THE MESSAGE

JESUS HELPS US PERSEVERE IN THE RACE OF FAITH.

He was the "team dad." The year his daughter ran high school cross-country, he brought a tent and a cooler full of drinks to every single meet. But he brought something more important than shade and electrolytes: He brought encouragement. He positioned himself throughout the course, darting back and forth in order to cheer the runners on at different points in the race.

Jesus goes above and beyond even the best team dad, because He has run the race before us. Having run the distance on the cross, He now cheers for us, enabling and supporting us in the race. When we keep our eyes on Him, we're sure to cross the finish line with victory and joy.

33

I tell you the truth, anyone who has faith in me will do
what I have been doing. He will do even greater things than these,
because I am going to the Father.

JOHN 14:12

JESUS GIVES US THE POWER TO CARRY ON HIS WORK.

Unquestionably, Jesus did amazing things during His earthly ministry. He healed the sick and raised the dead; He comforted and confronted and consoled.

What's even more amazing, though, is that He has instructed us to continue His work on earth. We have been given the honor and responsibility of proclaiming the gospel—the message of God's saving, healing, restoring love—to a lost and hurting world. And we don't have to do this on our own strength and resources: Jesus has promised us the Holy Spirit to guide, direct, and empower us as we continue His ministry.

As we follow Jesus closely and humbly, we witness—and participate in—His miracles.

34

It is for freedom that Christ has set us free.

GALATIANS 5:1A

JESUS GIVES US THE GIFT OF FREEDOM.

We have all played the role of the Pharisee. We pile up stacks of our good deeds, hoping to somehow reach God through our own merits. Before long, we become slaves to the impossible standards we set in our minds.

Such is the way of the law. The way of grace is different. The way of grace is to put our trust in Christ's sacrifice, not our own righteousness, to bring us to God. When we do that, we experience freedom; our hearts and minds are unchained to rules and guilt.

The way of the law is slavery, because no one can keep the law perfectly. The way of grace is freedom.

35

Jesus' priesthood is permanent. He's there from now to eternity
to save everyone who comes to God through him.
HEBREWS 7:24–25 THE MESSAGE

JESUS INTERCEDES FOR US.

The apostle John writes, "My dear children, I write this to you
so that you will not sin. But if anybody does sin, we have one
who speaks to the Father in our defense—Jesus Christ, the
Righteous One" (1 John 2:1).

Jesus is our advocate. He speaks to the Father on our behalf,
interceding for us, His blood cleansing us. He speaks for us as
a lawyer speaks to a judge. And Jesus is uniquely qualified for
such a role: His righteousness matches God the Father's.

We could never ask for a more faithful intercessor than Jesus
Christ the Righteous, the One who lives forever to intercede
for us.

36

Surely he has borne our griefs and carried our sorrows.
ISAIAH 53:4A NKJV

JESUS TAKES ON OUR PROBLEMS AND PAIN.

It's no secret that Jesus suffered—horribly. As God made man, He suffered the mundane afflictions we all face—tired feet, bruises, hunger and thirst. But He also endured one of the most physically taxing tortures ever devised, death on a cross.

What would motivate Jesus to endure that kind of pain? The answer is found in His great love for us. He suffered in our place, enduring pain that would bring us healing. And in a mysterious but very real way, the punishment He endured brings us peace.

Jürgen Moltmann writes, "Good Friday is the most comprehensive and most profound expression of Christ's fellowship with every human being." One of the most beautiful things about Jesus is that He suffers with and for us.

37

We love because he first loved us.
1 JOHN 4:19

JESUS INITIATES A RELATIONSHIP WITH US.

Love is a risky thing. There's always the possibility that the beloved will reject the lover, or that their love will fall apart when they discover that the other isn't perfect.

Fortunately for us, Jesus made the first move on the cross, drawing us to Himself and making it possible for us to live in relationship with Him. And His love for us is based not on our lovability but on His loving character.

As J. I. Packer writes, "All my knowledge of Him depends on His sustained initiative in knowing me. . . . He knows me as a friend, One who loves me." Our hearts are filled with joy when we realize that Jesus wants us to be His friend.

38

Christ loved the church and gave himself up for her to make her holy.
EPHESIANS 5:25B–26A

JESUS MAKES US HOLY.

Watch a mother with her toddler after he's just spent the afternoon making mud pies. She doesn't love him any less just because he's muddy. But she does set him in a bath and gently sponge off the layers of dirt, and then she gives him a fresh set of clothes.

In the same way, Jesus cleanses us, washing us and making us holy. He gives us a new set of clothes too—clothes of humility, compassion, gentleness, patience, and kindness, a far cry from our soiled suit of selfishness and pride.

Just like a good mom, Jesus loves us even when we're dirty. But He loves us too much to leave us that way.

39

For he has rescued us from the dominion of darkness and
brought us into the kingdom of the Son he loves,
in whom we have redemption, the forgiveness of sins.
COLOSSIANS 1:13–14

JESUS RESCUES US FROM A LIFE OF SIN.

The hostages, their senses dulled after months of prison and uncertainty, huddled in the dark. Suddenly, their consciousness was interrupted—noises, unfamiliar faces. It took them a minute to figure out what was going on, but soon they realized: They were being rescued. They had been found and were being led to safety.

We too once huddled in the darkness of our sin. And we too were rescued when Jesus came into our lives. He found us and led us to a better life—and His death on the cross provided a bridge to reach it. Jesus is our great Savior and Hero.

40

You have been given fullness in Christ,
who is the head over every power and authority.
COLOSSIANS 2:10B

JESUS GIVES US ACCESS TO THE ONE TRUE GOD.

Every now and then, something happens that makes us ask ourselves if our God is God enough. Can He handle our addictions? Can He heal our hearts? Can He protect us?

If we have put our trust in Jesus, the answer is a resounding yes. He is God over all—there is nothing that escapes His attention, and nothing is beyond His control. And He is "the Father of compassion and the God of all comfort, who comforts us in all our troubles, so that we can comfort those in any trouble" (2 Corinthians 1:3b–4b). He is in control of our lives, and His love and strength can be trusted even in the worst of times.

In Christ, we have all the God we could ever need.

41

In his great mercy he has given us new birth into a living hope through
the resurrection of Jesus Christ from the dead, and into an inheritance
that can never perish, spoil, or fade—kept in heaven for you.

1 PETER 1:3B–4

JESUS OFFERS US AN INHERITANCE THAT WILL NEVER SPOIL OR FADE.

There's a peace that comes to us when we know we're doing okay financially. Likewise, there's an anxiety that plagues our lives when we aren't quite sure how ends are going to meet. When we have money, we feel in control.

But Jesus tells us to store up treasure for ourselves "treasures in heaven, where moth and rust do not destroy, and where thieves do not break in and steal" (Matthew 6:20b). And Peter tells us that as part of our adoption as God's children, we have a heavenly inheritance that is incorruptible, untouchable.

This inheritance—and God's provision for us in general—is completely reliable, and brings a greater sense of assurance and peace than any amount of money.

Therefore he is able to save completely those who come to God through him, because he always lives to intercede for them.

HEBREWS 7:25

JESUS PRAYS FOR US.

We feel better when we share prayer requests—it's deeply comforting to know that friends and family are bringing our needs before God in prayer. It's amazing to think that Jesus does the same for us every day.

He prayed for us that we would be unified and know His love (John 17:20–23). He prayed for Simon, that his faith would not fail (Luke 22:32). Jesus knows us intimately and knows our needs better than we do. And, sitting at the right hand of the Father, He is more than able to bring our needs before Him with boldness.

It is indeed wonderful to be prayed for. And it's especially wonderful to be prayed for by the King of Kings Himself.

For God so loved the world that he gave his one and only Son, that
whoever believes in him shall not perish but have eternal life.

JOHN 3:16

JESUS GIVES US ETERNAL LIFE.

Jesus often talked about eternal life. And in John 17:3, He
tells us exactly what eternal life is when He prays, "Now this
is eternal life: that they may know you, the only true God, and
Jesus Christ, whom you have sent."

Eternal life is knowing God, and Jesus is how God makes
Himself known. Jesus came to reveal God—"Anyone who
has seen me has seen the Father," He told His disciple Philip
(John 14:9b). He is the Word of God (John 1:1) and the exact
representation of God's character (Hebrews 1:3).

Eternal life is life in light of God's presence, and Jesus brought
the presence of God near and available to us.

44

I have set you an example that you should do as I have done for you.
JOHN 13:15

JESUS SHOWS US HOW TO LIVE.

Godliness isn't exactly in our nature—looking to the interests of others is difficult, turning the other cheek next to impossible.

Fortunately, in Jesus we have a model, someone who shows us how to serve others and love God. Just as a child grows up watching his father and develops his habits and values, when we imitate Jesus, we grow to develop His love and compassion, His set of priorities. Watching Him wash His disciples' feet and adopting that same attitude of humility in our own relationships, we become like Him, spreading the beauty of Jesus throughout the world.

45

When two or three of you are together because of me,
you can be sure that I'll be there.
MATTHEW 18:20 THE MESSAGE

JESUS MEETS WITH US.

There are some groups that are never quite the same when the leader isn't present. A good leader brings a sense of dynamism and enthusiasm to a meeting and makes his flock feel energized and safe.

Jesus, of course, is the perfect Shepherd, a truly great leader. And even though He is no longer physically present, we have the promise that when we meet with other believers, He is there. He is there, as surely as if He were sitting next to us, to strengthen and speak to us through others and use us to strengthen and speak to them.

Anytime we get together, we have the promise of a very important Guest.

46

He calls his own sheep by name and leads them out.

JOHN 10:3B

JESUS KNOWS US BY NAME.

How long could you go without hearing someone say your name? A week? An hour? At some point, you would break down, desperate to know that someone was speaking directly to you.

When Jesus met Nathanael, He said, "Here is a true Israelite, in whom there is nothing false" (John 1:47b). Nathanael was awed that Jesus knew him without ever having met him—and the same awe overtakes us when we realize that He knows us that well too. He knows us and calls us by name.

Jesus gives us the opportunity to see and know God. But He also gives us the opportunity to be known by Him.

Jesus answered, "Everyone who drinks this water will be thirsty again, but whoever drinks the water I give him will never thirst. Indeed, the water I give him will become in him a spring of water welling up to eternal life."

JOHN 4:13–14

JESUS QUENCHES OUR DEEPEST THIRSTS.

Our bodies desperately need water. When we have enough water in our system, we feel more content physically and more able to focus mentally. No matter how much water we drink, though, sooner or later we're going to feel thirsty again.

When Jesus was on earth, He stood next to a well with a Samaritan woman and told her He could offer water that would end her thirst for good. Today, His offer is the same— streams of new life welling up within us, renewing our spirit and satisfying our most deeply felt thirsts. And with the water Jesus gives, we'll never thirst again.

48

Accept one another, then, just as Christ accepted you,
in order to bring praise to God.

ROMANS 15:7

JESUS ACCEPTS US.

The jury is still out on how many hugs we need in order to be healthy—studies suggest anywhere from four to twelve per day. Whatever the number, all of us need a simple embrace every now and then, an expression of acceptance and love.

In Jesus, God our Father runs toward us, the prodigal, and embraces us. It's not that we are sinless. It's that He is merciful. And by His mercy, we are able to live our lives in an embrace with God.

49

Ask and it will be given to you; seek and you will find; knock and the door will be opened to you. For everyone who asks receives; he who seeks finds; and to him who knocks, the door will be opened.

LUKE 11:9B–10

JESUS IS FOUND BY US WHEN WE SEEK HIM.

Throughout history, people have found the meaning of the universe to be elusive. For some, finding God is achieved only by climbing a ladder of enlightenment, with success always just beyond reach.

But in Jesus, God came down and lived with us. He wanted to be seen and known. Paul told the Athenians, "God did this so that men would seek him and perhaps reach out for him and find him, though he is not far from each one of us" (Acts 17:27).

God wants to be found by us. He "rewards those who earnestly seek him" (Hebrews 11:6b). And Jesus promises that if we continue to ask and seek and knock, we will be rewarded.

50

If we confess our sin, he is faithful and just and
will purify us from all unrighteousness.

1 JOHN 1:9

JESUS CLEANSES US FROM SIN.

The third graders were excited. Their teacher had set up a water purification system in their classroom, complete with charcoal and cotton filters, and they were headed outside to collect some puddle water to purify. After processing the water two or three times, it went from brown to faintly yellow. But it was still a far cry from the crystal-clear water that came out of the drinking fountain.

When we confess our sins to Jesus, He forgives them and removes the stain they leave on our souls. More powerful than any filtering system, He is able to purify our murky hearts, leaving them crystal clear.

51

I no longer call you servants, because a servant does not know his
master's business. Instead, I have called you friends, for everything
that I learned from my Father I have made known to you.

JOHN 15:15

JESUS CALLS US HIS FRIENDS.

Picked last. There's nothing worse. And if you're a less-than-stellar athlete, you have one hope: If one of your friends is a team captain, he might pick you early in the rotation. There's no feeling of relief quite like being chosen.

When we meet Jesus, we experience that sense of chosenness, because He chooses us—"You did not choose me, but I chose you and appointed you to go and bear fruit—fruit that will last" (John 15:16a). And He chooses us not to be His employees or even acquaintances, but His friends, His companions. Jesus' greatest gift to us is His friendship.

52

This is how God showed his love among us: He sent his one and only Son into the world that we might live through him.

1 JOHN 4:9

JESUS SHOWS US THE FATHER'S LOVE.

God, being God, possesses some qualities that we will never be able to fully understand. We will never understand His perfect wisdom or His incredible might. And it's certainly hard for us to understand His great love. "The love of God is greater far than tongue or pen could ever tell," goes the hymn.

Jesus, elevated on the cross, is the ultimate symbol of God's love for us—"But God demonstrates his own love for us in this: While we were still sinners, Christ died for us," Paul says (Romans 5:8). And Jesus still speaks to us, reminding us of how much the Father loves us. Praise God for loving us enough to save us through Christ.

53

But he was pierced for our transgressions,
he was crushed for our iniquities;
the punishment that brought us peace was upon him,
and by his wounds we are healed.

ISAIAH 53:5

JESUS BRINGS US HEALING.

Scripture teaches us that all of creation is under a curse, and we feel it every day—death, disease, suffering. But Jesus died to redeem creation, to buy it back from death and destruction. When He was ministering on earth, He healed the sick and raised the dead, restorative power pouring from His hands to comfort and make well.

Because of His great sacrifice, we experience healing and have the promise that all things will work together for good in our lives (Romans 8:28). In Jesus, God is able to take our darkest days and bleakest circumstances and redeem them, making them beautiful.

54

You have this faith and love because of your hope, and what you hope
for is kept safe for you in heaven. You learned about this hope when you
heard the message about the truth, the Good News.

COLOSSIANS 1:5 NCV

JESUS GIVES US THE HOPE OF HEAVEN.

We're not quite sure what heaven will be like. What will
we do there? Will people look the same—will we be able to
recognize friends?

We do know, however, that heaven will be wonderful. God will
wipe the tears from the eyes of the persecuted; He will give
justice to the oppressed. There will be a new heaven and a
new earth, and all that's wrong will be made right.

Jesus enriches our earthly lives in so many ways, but "if only
for this life we have hope in Christ, we are to be pitied more
than all men" (1 Corinthians 15:19). So firm, so sure is the
promise of heaven that it gives us an unshakeable hope for
our present life.

55

For he himself is our peace.
EPHESIANS 2:14A

JESUS GIVES US PEACE WITH OTHERS.

Ask any marriage expert what the keys to a lasting relationship are, and forgiveness will probably top the list. In order to live with others in close relationship, we need forgiveness and kindness to grease the wheels.

Jesus is our model for forgiveness and a servant's heart. He forgives us, insisting that we show the same grace to others, and teaches us to serve those around us. The peace that comes to us when we experience His forgiveness makes it easier for us to forgive. And His love frees us from the anxiety and fear that so often create strife in our relationships.

Having Jesus in our lives enables us to bear with others the way He bears with us.

56

So if the Son sets you free, you will be free indeed.

JOHN 8:36

JESUS GIVES US TRUE FREEDOM.

Jean-Jacques Rousseau once wrote, "Man is born free, but everywhere he is in chains." Many of us live free from political and social slavery, and yet it's very possible to be completely free and yet still be a slave—a slave to sin, a slave to doubt, a slave to addiction.

When Jesus came, He challenged the religiously comfortable. They claimed to be sons of Abraham, not slaves; but their hearts were still slaves to sin. If the Son set them free, Jesus told them, they would be truly free—free in their hearts and in their relationship with their Father.

When Jesus sets us free, we are completely, truly free from the things that enslave our souls.

57

You may ask me for anything in my name, and I will do it.

JOHN 14:14

JESUS HEARS OUR PRAYERS.

Imagine being friends with someone, yet never talking. The relationship would probably fall apart.

As part of His relationship with His Father, Jesus made communication a habit—He rose early to pray and commune with God. And He offers us the same privilege of prayer, a freedom between us and God, the ability to come to Him with all our requests and petitions, along with the promise that He will hear us.

Jesus' promise to answer prayers made in His name presupposes closeness with Him and familiarity with His purposes. The easy communication we experience in prayer is a result of Jesus' amazing gift of friendship.

58

A bruised reed he will not break, and a smoldering wick
he will not snuff out, till he leads justice to victory.

MATTHEW 12:20

JESUS IS COMPASSIONATE TO THOSE WHO ARE HURTING.

When Jesus came to earth, He came to seek and save what was lost, to heal and restore. As He went about this mission, He came across people who desperately needed that restoration, who were crying out for God's mercy.

One such person was the widow at Nain. When Jesus encountered a funeral procession and saw a widow grieving the loss of her only son—and thus her future—"his heart went out to her and he said, 'Don't cry'" (Luke 7:13b). Then He touched the coffin and raised her son, and "gave him back to his mother" (7:15b).

Ours is not a task-driven, utilitarian Savior. Jesus' heart beats with compassion for the people He came to save, and He treats the hurting with special care.

But when the time had fully come, God sent his Son,
born of a woman, born under law, to redeem those under law,
that we might receive the full rights of sons.

GALATIANS 4:4–5

JESUS REDEEMS US.

When the Israelites rose up out of the slavery of Egypt,
they sang songs and described their exodus in terms of
"redemption"—being set free from the bondage they had
known, receiving a new, free life.

In the same way, Jesus redeems us. He sets us free from the
bondage of sin and gives us a new life. In Jesus, we are no
longer slaves but sons and daughters, children of God: "And
because you are children, God has sent the Spirit of his Son
into our hearts, crying, 'Abba! Father!'" (Galatians 4:6 NRSV).
By dying on the cross, Jesus bought us out of slavery, and we
now worship God as His beloved children.

60

But seek first his kingdom and his righteousness,
and all these things will be given to you as well.

MATTHEW 6:33

JESUS TAKES CARE OF US.

Jesus had some tough things to say about following Him. He
said it was easier for a camel to go through the eye of a needle
than for a rich man to enter the kingdom of God. He said that
anyone who loved his father or mother more than Him was
not worthy of Him.

But He also said that the hairs on our heads are all numbered,
and that "no one who has left home or wife or brothers or
parents or children for the sake of the kingdom of God will
fail to receive many times as much in this age and, in the
age to come, eternal life" (Luke 18:29b–30). When we follow
Jesus and seek Him first, we are abundantly taken care of.

61

But you are a chosen people, a royal priesthood, a holy nation,
a people belonging to God, that you may declare the praises of him
who called you out of darkness into his wonderful light. Once you
were not a people, but now you are the people of God; once you
had not received mercy, but now you have received mercy.

1 PETER 2:9–10

JESUS GIVES US A NEW IDENTITY.

We all need to belong, and we can all think of a few times
when we did something we regretted just to identify with a
group.

With Jesus in our lives, we finally belong. We are accepted by
Him, and we also become part of a unique group. As believers,
we are freedom fighters, releasing the captives. We have been
given the ministry of reconciliation, charged with preaching
the message of God's saving love. No longer identified with
the darkness, we are identified as salt and light, overcoming
evil with good.

Our new identity in Christ gives our lives purpose, fulfillment,
and joy.

62

Now it is God who makes both us and you stand firm in Christ.
He anointed us, set his seal of ownership on us, and put his Spirit
in our hearts as a deposit, guaranteeing what is to come.

2 CORINTHIANS 1:21–22

JESUS ENABLES US
TO STAND FIRM.

The book of Hebrews tells us that our salvation is secure, that God's promises are completely steadfast: "We have this hope as an anchor for the soul, firm and secure" (6:19a).

Having Jesus as our anchor gives us an unshakeable hope. With His Spirit reassuring us of what God has done in our lives, we can know beyond a shadow of a doubt that the storms of our life can never truly harm us—they are no match for the One who has saved us.

In Christ, we can weather any storm. Come what may, we can persevere.

63

He chose what the world thinks is unimportant and what the
world looks down on and thinks is nothing in order to
destroy what the world thinks is important.

1 CORINTHIANS 1:28 NCV

JESUS USES US AS WE ARE,
EVEN IN OUR WEAKNESS.

The boy couldn't race. A quadriplegic, there was no way
he could compete in a cycling event, even though it was a
longtime dream of his. So his father bought a special bike,
and together the two finished the race, the dad sweating as he
carried his son over the finish line.

Just like a good dad, Jesus doesn't take us out of the race
because of our inabilities. He works in and through us and
carries us over the finish line. Our imperfections become an
asset in His hands, a way to reveal His glory and strength.

Jesus doesn't need our perfection or our strength. He just
needs our willingness to join our lives with His.

64

In my Father's house are many rooms; if it were not so, I would
have told you. I am going there to prepare a place for you.

JOHN 14:2

JESUS IS PREPARING A PLACE FOR US.

Anytime we've been away from loved ones, we miss them. We
wish we could see their faces, not in a photo, but in person.
We want to be in their presence.

In the same way, we "miss" God. We experience His presence,
but we wish we could finally see Him face to face. The good
news is that Jesus is preparing a place where we can be with
God. When we are finally ushered into His presence, we will
worship Him without the veil of the physical world.

As the psalmist said: "You have made known to me the
path of life; you will fill me with joy in your presence, with
eternal pleasures at your right hand" (Psalm 16:11). In God's
presence, we will find great joy.

65

Let the peace of Christ rule in your hearts,
since as members of one body you were called to peace.
COLOSSIANS 3:15A

JESUS GIVES US UNITY.

Lots of things separate us from others—geography, preferences, backgrounds, languages. Sometimes it's easier to pick out what's different about us than what we have in common.

The early church felt the same kind of division between Jewish Christians and the new Gentile converts. But as Paul told the Ephesians, Jesus knit the two together; He "destroyed the barrier, the dividing wall of hostility" (Ephesians 2:14b). We are all reconciled to God in Christ, and thereby reconciled to each other.

When we remember what Jesus has done in our lives and celebrate what He has done in the lives of others, the walls between us slowly dissolve, and we experience unity and peace.

66

May our Lord Jesus Christ himself and God our Father encourage you
and strengthen you in every good thing you do and say.

2 THESSALONIANS 2:16 NCV

JESUS ENCOURAGES US.

To "encourage" someone is to give them courage, confidence, and boldness. And Jesus is one of the best encouragers of all.

Sometimes it's a word of thanks spoken by someone we've helped. Sometimes it's a financial miracle that lets us know that He is behind us in our endeavors. Sometimes it's a hug from a friend or a note from a loved one. Whatever form it takes, when we seek to serve Jesus, His encouragement follows us wherever we go.

We may not know when or how, but we do know that Jesus provides us with all the strength and courage we need for every good work.

Some friends play at friendship
but a true friend sticks closer than one's nearest kin.
PROVERBS 18:24 NRSV

JESUS IS A FAITHFUL FRIEND.

When it comes to the big things in life, there is no substitute for family. "In time of test, family is best," goes the proverb. Although no family is perfect, it's family who stand beside us at the gravesite. Family helps us move. Family is the first to know when a new baby enters the world.

And yet Jesus is even more faithful than our dearest family members. His faithfulness and consistency are unsurpassed. He is never fickle toward us. When we are world-weary, He lifts our burdens and gives us what we need to keep going.

Life is incomplete without family and friends who feel like family. And Jesus is the best Friend of all.

68

He who began a good work in you will carry it on to
completion until the day of Christ Jesus.

PHILIPPIANS 1:6B

JESUS MAKES US BETTER PEOPLE.

Some couples are "odd." We're not quite sure why she would date someone like him. But he will inevitably say about her, "She makes me a better person." Being with her raises the standards to which he holds himself, and he becomes more couth, more considerate, and more engaging.

In the same way, when we have an awareness of Jesus' presence—and He is with us always—it raises our standards. We feel a desire to represent Him well, to "live a life worthy of the calling [we] have received" (Ephesians 4:1b). And with His Spirit and transforming presence at work in our lives, we slowly become more patient, more consistent, and more loving—more like Him.

69

As a mother comforts her child, so will I comfort you.

ISAIAH 66:13A

JESUS COMFORTS US.

Comfort may take many forms—chicken soup when we're sick, flowers when we're grieving, a hug when we didn't get that job. One of the things that help us most when we're in need of comfort is simply *words*: Hearing comforting words spoken gives us hope that we can get beyond our struggle.

When Jesus' disciples needed comfort, He spoke to them. He said He would hear their prayers and that He had overcome the world. He told them not to let their hearts be troubled. He said that the Counselor would come and remind them of what He had said to them.

And Jesus' words remain with us today, giving us comfort and strength.

70

> All this is from God, who reconciled us to himself through
> Christ and gave us the ministry of reconciliation.
>
> 2 CORINTHIANS 5:18

JESUS MAKES US HIS AMBASSADORS.

An ambassador is a representative, a messenger. Jesus has charged us with the task of being His ambassadors, to "make disciples of all nations" (Matthew 28:19b).

Representing Jesus to all nations seems like a stiff challenge. But Jesus gives us His presence (Matthew 28:20) and the Holy Spirit to embolden us (Acts 1:8). Plus, He gives us things to talk about: Declaring the goodness of Jesus becomes easier when we reflect on everything He has done for us.

Psalm 105:1 says, "Give thanks to the LORD, call on his name; make known among the nations what he has done." Through Christ, God has done amazing things in our lives, and He wants us to let the whole world know.

For what I received I passed on to you as of first importance:
that Christ died for our sins according to the Scriptures.

1 CORINTHIANS 15:3

JESUS TAKES OUR PUNISHMENT UPON HIMSELF.

At the Last Supper, Jesus gathered His disciples with Him. He broke the bread and told them to take it and eat it, saying, "This is my body given for you; do this in remembrance of me" (Luke 22:19b). The next chapter of Luke finds Jesus crucified—for us.

John Stott writes, "Man claims prerogatives that belong to God alone; God accepts penalties which belong to man alone." Jesus' death on the cross accomplished our forgiveness, our redemption, our being made whole. Only because He died in our place, allowing His body to be broken for us, are we able to experience salvation.

I press on toward the goal to win the prize for which
God has called me heavenward in Christ Jesus.

PHILIPPIANS 3:14

JESUS REWARDS OUR EFFORTS.

When we work out, we want to see a payoff—more definition,
greater endurance, more energy. Otherwise, we start to lose
motivation. Likewise, in our spiritual workout efforts, we can
sometimes get bogged down, wondering if it's all really worth
it.

In Jesus' parable of the talents, He reminds us that God
rewards our efforts to multiply what He has given us. And
James reminds us that when we persevere, we grow in
maturity and character (James 1:4). When we run after Jesus,
we are assured that we will receive the prize we are seeking.
In James's words, "Blessed is the man who perseveres under
trial, because when he has stood the test, he will receive the
crown of life that God has promised to those who love him"
(1:12).

For whoever exalts himself will be humbled,
and whoever humbles himself will be exalted.
MATTHEW 23:12

JESUS LIFTS UP THE HUMBLE.

He's easy to pick out in any teen movie: the jerk. Cocky and proud, the jerk torments the protagonist with verbal and physical jabs until his day of comeuppance, usually near the end of the movie.

We all hate the jerk. And yet there's a little jerk in all of us. All of us exalt ourselves and put others down sometimes, hogging the spotlight or making others feel bad about themselves. And very often, our pride earns us a painful comeuppance.

Jesus values humility and reserves exaltation for the humble. When we adopt His attitude of humility—when we put others above ourselves and acknowledge that we need God's grace and strength—we experience His blessings.

74

You have begun to live the new life, in which you are being
made new and are becoming like the One who made you.
This new life brings you the true knowledge of God.

COLOSSIANS 3:10 NCV

JESUS GIVES US KNOWLEDGE OF GOD.

Everyone loves a celebrity sighting. When we catch a glimpse
of our favorite singer at a restaurant or spy our favorite actor
walking down the street, we're quick to call our friends.

In Jesus, God offers us the opportunity not just to catch a
little glimpse of Him, but to know Him. Jesus reveals to us
God's character and tells us what He's like—His motivations
and personality and values. More than just knowledge about
God, though, Jesus offers the opportunity to really know God,
to relate to Him as closely as we relate to our friends and
family. Because of Jesus, God is not a faraway celebrity we see
every now and then; He becomes *our* God, our Friend.

75

Grace and peace to you from God our Father and the Lord Jesus Christ,
who gave himself for our sins to rescue us from the present evil age,
according to the will of our God and Father.

GALATIANS 1:3–4

JESUS GIVES UP HIS LIFE FOR US.

Love is often measured by the sacrifices we make for our loved one. But most of us never have the opportunity to make great sacrifices. We may skip a TV show to take a friend to the airport or give up a hot shower to let a family member get ready first, but most of us will never sacrifice a kidney or even a whole day of our lives.

Jesus told His disciples, "Greater love has no one than this, that he lay down his life for his friends" (John 15:13). And that's exactly what He did for us: He laid down His life so that we might live. Because of His love for us, Jesus gave us everything He could possibly give—right up to His own life.

Forgetting what is behind and straining toward what is ahead,
I press on toward the goal to win the prize for which God
has called me heavenward in Christ Jesus.

PHILIPPIANS 3:13B–14

JESUS FREES US FROM OUR PAST.

The apostle Paul had a past: Before becoming a Christian, he zealously persecuted the Church. But rather than deny it or cover it up, he said, "For I am the least of the apostles and do not even deserve to be called an apostle, because I persecuted the church of God. But by the grace of God I am what I am" (1 Corinthians 15:9–10a).

Simone Weil writes, "It is sometimes easy to deliver an unhappy person from his present distress, but it is difficult to set him free from his past affliction. Only God can do it." Some of us are running away from the past, trying to escape it. But Jesus' grace offers us the ability to accept the past and embrace the future—His grace restores us and gives us joy.

In him we have redemption through his blood, the forgiveness of sins,
in accordance with the riches of God's grace that he lavished
on us with all wisdom and understanding.

EPHESIANS 1:7–8

JESUS OFFERS US FORGIVENESS AND GRACE.

All we know about her is that she had lived "a sinful life." She was not worthy, they murmured, to touch the feet of the Rabbi, much less kiss them and anoint them with perfume. Instead of brushing her aside, though, Jesus affirmed her offering and said, "Your sins are forgiven. . . . Your faith has saved you; go in peace" (Luke 7:48, 50).

When they heard the word "forgiven," the murmuring began again: "Who is this who even forgives sins?" (7:49b). In that grace-filled moment, they knew that the man among them was not just a prophet, that He had the power even to forgive sins.

Today Jesus offers us the same moment of grace, saying to us, "You are forgiven. Go in peace."

When Jesus spoke again to the people, he said,
"I am the light of the world. Whoever follows me will never
walk in darkness, but will have the light of life."

JOHN 8:12

JESUS BRINGS LIGHT TO THE WORLD.

Poverty-stricken areas of town can be bleak and depressing—broken windows, broken down cars, broken down lives. Before too long, everything feels hopeless. But even the tiniest sign of life—a pot of flowers, a fresh coat of paint, a smiling face—can be a beacon of hope.

Jesus came to bring light and life to this hurting, broken down world. Where He is—where there are signs of His compassion and willingness to reach out to the most seemingly lost soul—there is hope. When we, His followers, send out signs of His life, we give hope to those around us.

79

To him who is able to keep you from falling and to present you before his glorious presence without fault and with great joy—to the only God our Savior be glory, majesty, power and authority, through Jesus Christ our Lord, before all ages, now and forevermore! Amen.

JUDE 24–25

JESUS PICKS US UP WHEN WE FALL DOWN.

It seemed like an only mildly dangerous cave tour—until about two-thirds of the way through, when a largish man became stuck in a narrow tunnel. He panicked, his chest expanding, which only made the problem worse. So the cave guide and other tourists calmed him down, and he was able to squeeze through. If he'd been alone, the afternoon could have ended much differently.

Ecclesiastes 4:10a says, "If one falls down, his friend can help him up," and Jesus is that Friend for us. He picks us up with His wisdom and grace when we make a mistake or experience a setback. When we walk with Him, the stumbles and bumbles in our faith and life need not be fatal.

Jesus answered, "I am the way and the truth and the life.
No one comes to the Father except through me."

JOHN 14:6

JESUS SHOWS US THE TRUTH.

Most great stories are about searching for truth and finding it in unexpected places. We see ourselves in those who are seeking to understand something true about the world and themselves, and we envy them when they experience moments of revelation.

The search for truth is a universal one, and truth often seems to slip through our grasp. But Jesus tells us that He is the truth—He is the ultimate revelation about the world, the human condition, and the God who saves. "The Word was God. . . . The Word became flesh and blood, and moved into the neighborhood," John writes (John 1:1b, 14 THE MESSAGE). In Jesus, the truth of God has come near. Because of Jesus, we can know the truth.

And will not God bring about justice for his chosen ones,
who cry out to him day and night? Will he keep putting them off?

LUKE 18:7

JESUS HEARS US WHEN WE CRY FOR HELP.

Bartimaeus was not doing well in life—he was blind, and he was a beggar. So when he heard that Jesus was passing along, he cried out to Him for help, shouting, "Jesus, Son of David, have mercy on me!" (Mark 10:47b). Jesus stopped. He told the crowd to call Bartimaeus near to Him, where the blind man received his sight.

But he received more than just physical sight: His spiritual eyes were opened, and he became a follower of Jesus. Jesus heard his cry for physical help and saw through to his spiritual condition.

Anytime we call on Jesus for help, we should expect to receive far more than we asked for.

82

No temptation has seized you except what is common to man.
And God is faithful; he will not let you be tempted
beyond what you can bear. But when you are tempted,
he will also provide a way out so that you can stand up under it.
1 CORINTHIANS 10:13

JESUS ENABLES US TO ENDURE TEMPTATION.

It always shocks us when we suddenly face a bout with temptation. The quickened heartbeat, the indecision, the feeling of impending guilt—no one enjoys being tempted.

Fortunately for us, we have a Savior who knows all about temptation, because He was tempted Himself. Before He began His ministry, Jesus retreated into the desert to fast and pray, where He was tempted three times. Each time, just like us, He had to consciously choose what He knew was right.

Hebrews 4:15 says, "For we do not have a high priest who is unable to sympathize with our weaknesses, but we have one who has been tempted in every way, just as we are—yet was without sin." Because Jesus overcame temptation, He is able to help us fight against the temptations we face each day.

The people were amazed at his teaching, because he taught them as one
who had authority, not as the teachers of the law.

MARK 1:22

JESUS TEACHES US.

Henry Brooks Adams once said, "A teacher affects eternity;
he can never tell where his influence stops." A good teacher
can make a world of difference in a student's life.

Jesus is an exemplary teacher. He is completely wise—nothing
surprises Him, nothing is beyond His realm of expertise. He
is also completely patient and humble, and He knows just
how much of a challenge we can handle. When we allow Jesus
to teach us, we grow in both wisdom and character.

When Jesus taught in the Capernaum synagogue, everyone
was amazed at His wisdom and authority. As God and man,
Jesus is the best, most qualified teacher we could ever have.

84

I am the Vine, you are the branches. When you're joined with me and
I with you, the relation intimate and organic, the harvest is sure to be
abundant. Separated, you can't produce a thing.

JOHN 15:5 THE MESSAGE

JESUS PRODUCES FRUIT IN OUR LIVES.

Sometimes we view living as one of Christ's followers as sort of
like being an independent consultant: Jesus is the "company,"
and we work for Him out of our homes, trying to maintain a
certain level of performance. We receive resources, but only
by mail or on occasional face-to-face meetings.

In reality, the truly saved life is a connected life, a life that
flows directly out of loving connection with Jesus. We aren't
expected to achieve results without Him—nor are we even
able to. It's as we meet with Him daily that we receive our
sense of mission and the resources we need to accomplish it.

Connecting with Jesus is connecting with the only true source
of life.

Then Jesus declared, "I am the bread of life. He who comes to me will never go hungry, and he who believes in me will never be thirsty."

JOHN 6:35

JESUS GIVES US THE BREAD OF LIFE.

As the Israelites wandered in the desert toward the Promised Land, they grumbled. What would they eat? What would they drink? So God provided manna, bread from heaven, each day—a symbol of God's faithful, unwavering provision for their needs.

Jesus declared Himself to be the true manna, the Bread of Life. He is the ultimate fulfillment of God's provision and blessing. "[God] humbled you, causing you to hunger and then feeding you with manna, which neither you nor your fathers had known," Deuteronomy 8:3 tells us, "to teach you that man does not live on bread alone but on every word that comes from the mouth of the LORD." Jesus the Bread of Life ultimately, eternally satisfies our hunger for the word of God.

I consider my life worth nothing to me, if only I may finish
the race and complete the task the Lord Jesus has given me—
the task of testifying to the gospel of God's grace.

ACTS 20:24

JESUS MAKES OUR LIVES AN ADVENTURE.

There are two ways to play any sport. The first is to get the ball as often as you can, shoot all you can, and make all the tackles you can. The second is to lay low, hoping the ball never comes within five yards of you. The second is preferred by the more athletically challenged among us. But the first is more fun.

Knowing Jesus gives us the opportunity to live our lives the first way. He gives us purpose and passion. He gives us skills. And He gives us a very important role in the coming Kingdom.

Even if we can't catch or throw, Jesus makes us impact players for His glory.

87

When Jesus landed and saw a large crowd,
he had compassion on them and healed their sick.

MATTHEW 14:14

JESUS DOES MIRACLES IN OUR LIVES.

We don't know how it got that way, but the man's right hand was shriveled and useless. Who knows how long it had held him back, how many times it had brought the blush of shame to his face? And so, when Jesus saw him, despite the mutterings of the Pharisees who wanted to see if He would heal on the Sabbath, Jesus restored the man's hand (Luke 6:6–11). Good as new.

Jesus' miracles tell us many things. They display God's power and reveal the nature of the Kingdom Jesus brings about. They also show that God is concerned with our needs. It's as true now as it was in the first century: Jesus cares, and He intervenes in our lives in miraculous ways.

88

His mercy extends to those who fear him,
from generation to generation.

LUKE 1:50

JESUS GIVES US HIS MERCY.

The ancient prayer goes, "Lord Jesus Christ, Son of God, have mercy upon me, a sinner." When we pray that prayer, we're modeling ourselves after the tax collector in Jesus' parable, casting ourselves on the Father's mercy; we're praying for forgiveness and that God would reach down and meet our needs.

The mercy that Jesus gives looks like seeking out lost sheep, forgiving great debts, doing good to one's enemies, and running after a long lost son. When we look for them, we see His mercies—His loving-kindnesses and compassion—abundantly in our lives.

By this all men will know that you are my disciples,
if you love one another.

JOHN 13:35

JESUS TEACHES US HOW TO LOVE.

Love is confusing. Nevertheless, two things are obvious: We all desperately need love, and few of us are particularly good at loving.

It's true that we could all use love lessons. We're a little bit selfish; we forget to consider the love needs of others. And sometimes we simply don't know how to show love.

Thankfully, we have Jesus to model love for us—the sacrifice, the investment of time, the giving and serving. We also have His Spirit to quicken the love in our hearts for others: "The fruit of the Spirit is love" (Galatians 5:22a). And as we grow in love with our Savior, we show the world what His love is like and glorify God.

I have been crucified with Christ and I no longer live, but Christ lives
in me. The life I live in the body, I live by faith in the Son of God,
who loved me and gave himself for me.

GALATIANS 2:20

JESUS LIVES IN US.

Paul first encountered Jesus on the road to Damascus. After that, he made such a turnaround that he even changed his name—Saul, the persecutor of Christians, became Paul, one of the Church's foremost apostles.

Later, he wrote to the Galatians, "I no longer live, but Christ lives in me. The life I live in the body, I live by faith in the Son of God" (2:20b). So complete and all-encompassing was that encounter with Christ that it affected every part of his being.

Just as it did for Paul, the new life we have in Christ touches our minds, souls, and bodies. He becomes part of us. And we are never the same.

91

Now the tax collectors and "sinners" were all gathering around to hear
him. But the Pharisees and the teachers of the law muttered,
"This man welcomes sinners and eats with them."

LUKE 15:1–2

JESUS NOTICES THE OUTCASTS.

Some people are simply "invisible" to many of us: lunchroom
nerds, eccentric neighbors, friends-of-friends with checkered
pasts . . . underfed, overworked children on the other side of
the world.

The people we tend to notice the least are the people Jesus
notices most. While He was on earth, He spent time with
people who were largely rejected in their time: He heard the
cry of lepers and healed them; He ate with tax collectors and
sinners; He chatted with Samaritan women.

The good news for us today is that when we feel like an
outcast, we know that He sees us and reaches out for us. And
as we experience His compassion, He gives us His eyes to
notice the outcasts all around us.

92

He too shared in their humanity so that by his death he might destroy him who holds the power of death—that is, the devil—and free those who all their lives were held in slavery by their fear of death.

HEBREWS 2:14B–15

JESUS OVERCOMES THE DEVIL.

Sin and death go together. They entered the world hand in hand, and where sin plagues our lives, death is its close companion. And both feed on the power of the devil.

But when Jesus took on our humanity, He also took on death by dying on the cross—and defeated it by rising from the dead. At the exact moment of His resurrection, the devil was defeated, sin and death along with him. And when we unite our lives with Christ's, we share in that victory as well. Because of Jesus, sin and death hold no power in our lives.

And God raised us up with Christ and seated us with him
in the heavenly realms in Christ Jesus.

EPHESIANS 2:6

JESUS GIVES US SECURITY.

When Jesus saved us, He reached down and took on everything that plagues us. He took on humanity, frail flesh itself, and the sin and death and disease that infect our lives. He jumped in the water in order to save us from drowning.

But in His resurrection, Jesus is exalted far above every weakness, everything that harms and threatens. Having defeated even death, He sits at the right hand of the Father, seated "in the heavenly realms" (Ephesians 2:6b). Even more than that, though, God has seated us with Him. In Christ, we are safe and secure from every enemy and power.

94

When you are brought before synagogues, rulers and authorities,
do not worry about how you will defend yourselves or what you will say,
for the Holy Spirit will teach you at that time what you should say.

LUKE 12:11–12

JESUS GIVES US COURAGE.

There comes a time in each of our lives when we have to choose to do the right thing. And the thing about the right thing is that it very often requires a lot of courage to do. It's not easy to take a stand against dishonesty at work or come clean to a friend about something we're ashamed of.

Scripture tells us that the Lord delights in those who do what is right. It pleases Jesus when we make right choices—and He gives us the courage to make those choices. He gives us the words to say, the opportunity to say them, and the guts it takes to follow through. Jesus gives us His courage, His strength, every time we need it.

95

Father, I want those you have given me to be with me where I am,
and to see my glory, the glory you have given me because you loved me
before the creation of the world.

JOHN 17:24

JESUS WANTS TO BE WITH US.

Invitations are a great thing to get in the mail, a break from the ho-hum of bills and advertisements. There's just something special and exciting about knowing that someone wants you to share in their wedding day or birthday celebration.

Jesus has sent us an invitation to witness His glory, to share in the love between Him and the Father. He invites us to join our lives with His. He wants to be near us; He wants to be a part of everything we're going through.

The invitation from Jesus to share in His life is the greatest honor we could ever receive.

96

For whoever wants to save his life will lose it,
but whoever loses his life for me will save it.

LUKE 9:24

JESUS CHALLENGES US.

Jesus' disciples were a unique group, hand picked by Him to be His closest companions, to learn from Him, and later to carry on His work. But that privilege didn't come without cost. Following Jesus meant complete commitment, complete willingness. Jesus said, "Anyone who loves his father or mother more than me is not worthy of me; anyone who loves his son or daughter more than me is not worthy of me" (Matthew 10:37).

His challenge is the same for us today: We must daily choose to follow Him if we want to be His disciples, even if it means giving up what's most important to us. The good news is that just as Jesus' disciples experienced blessing by responding to His challenges, so do we.

97

Therefore, if anyone is in Christ, he is a new creation;
the old has gone, the new has come!
2 CORINTHIANS 5:17

JESUS GIVES US A BRAND-NEW LIFE.

Some days, we feel bogged down in old habits, difficult circumstances, and a simple lack of energy. We wonder if we're living the life God intended for us.

On days like these, it's good to remember the day we first met Jesus. He flooded our lives with His love; it was like a light suddenly came on inside our souls, and we were brand new. And even though it may not feel like it every day, He has given us a new, full life in Him—in Christ, we are a completely new creation. And even now, God is working on us.

98

The Spirit of the Lord is on me, because he has anointed me to preach good news to the poor. He has sent me to proclaim freedom for the prisoners and recovery of sight for the blind, to release the oppressed, to proclaim the year of the Lord's favor.

LUKE 4:18–19

JESUS RESTORES US.

In many ways, Jesus turns everything we know about life on its head. Blessed are the poor, He says, the bereaved, and the meek, and in order to save our lives, we must lose them in Him. Jesus came to bring about God's justice, to set things right in the world. And that restoration still takes place in our lives today.

When we are poor, He blesses us. When we are hurt, He heals us. When we cry out to Him in mourning, He comforts us. When we are broken, Jesus puts us back together again.

99

God has said, "Never will I leave you; never will I forsake you."
HEBREWS 13:5B

JESUS STAYS WITH US.

There are times when we simply can't feel God's presence. All the Bible verses we have memorized feel hollow and empty. We feel like we've fallen off God's radar. The sky is silent, and we feel alone.

But even in our lonely times, we know that we're not really alone. Jesus has promised to be with us always, and He is completely faithful—"if we are faithless, he will remain faithful, for he cannot disown himself" (2 Timothy 2:13). And because He Himself experienced loneliness, He can identify with us in our lonely times.

Our lonely times will pass. And when they do, we will realize that Jesus was there all along.

Then he said to them all: "If anyone would come after me,
he must deny himself and take up his cross daily and follow me."
LUKE 9:23

JESUS MAKES EACH DAY MEANINGFUL.

"Today" is an important day throughout the Gospels. "Today" a Savior was born in the town of David. "Today" salvation came to the house of Zacchaeus. The thief on the cross met Jesus in paradise "today." In the middle of ordinary days on ordinary soil, Jesus walked the earth and spread God's grace.

When we have Jesus in our lives, each today becomes an opportunity to experience Him and live in His Kingdom, no matter how ordinary the day may seem. Today is an opportunity to follow Jesus. Today is a day to feel the warmth His grace. Because of Jesus, each day counts, and each day has meaning.

101

I always thank God for you because of his grace given you in Christ Jesus.

1 CORINTHIANS 1:4

JESUS GIVES US HIS GRACE.

We often hear the word "grace," but sometimes we're not quite sure what grace really is, what grace looks like. During Jesus' ministry, grace looked like forgiving a sinful woman; proclaiming God's favor and blessing on the poor in spirit, on the bereaved; freeing a demoniac from his physical and spiritual shackles; healing the sick.

Grace is simply the hand of God reaching out for us and blessing us, despite how much we don't deserve His blessing.

The life we have with God is not something we earned or deserved. It is Jesus' gift of grace.

Scripture Index

Scripture Index

101

I always thank God for you because of his grace given you in Christ Jesus.

1 CORINTHIANS 1:4

JESUS GIVES US HIS GRACE.

We often hear the word "grace," but sometimes we're not quite sure what grace really is, what grace looks like. During Jesus' ministry, grace looked like forgiving a sinful woman; proclaiming God's favor and blessing on the poor in spirit, on the bereaved; freeing a demoniac from his physical and spiritual shackles; healing the sick.

Grace is simply the hand of God reaching out for us and blessing us, despite how much we don't deserve His blessing.

The life we have with God is not something we earned or deserved. It is Jesus' gift of grace.